LIGHTNING BOLT BOOKS™

From Assembly Lines to Home Offices

How Work Has Changed

Jennifer Boothroyd

Lerner Publications Company

Minneapolis

For Gloria,
my mentor
and friend

Lerner Publications Company
A division of Lerner Publishing Group, Inc.
241 First Avenue North
Minneapolis, MN 55401 U.S.A.

Website address: www.lernerbooks.com

Library of Congress Cataloging-in-Publication Data

Boothroyd, Jennifer, 1972-
    From assembly lines to home offices : how work has changed / by Jennifer Boothroyd.
        p.   cm. — (Lightning bolt books™—Comparing past and present)
    Includes index.
    ISBN 978-0-7613-6748-2 (lib. bdg. : alk. paper)
    1. Work—Juvenile literature. 2. Labor—Juvenile literature. 3. Occupations—Juvenile
literature. I. Title.
    HD4902.5.B66 2012
    331—dc22   2011005067

Manufactured in the United States of America
1 – CG – 7/15/11

Contents

Work

Many people work at a job. They earn money for the work they do.

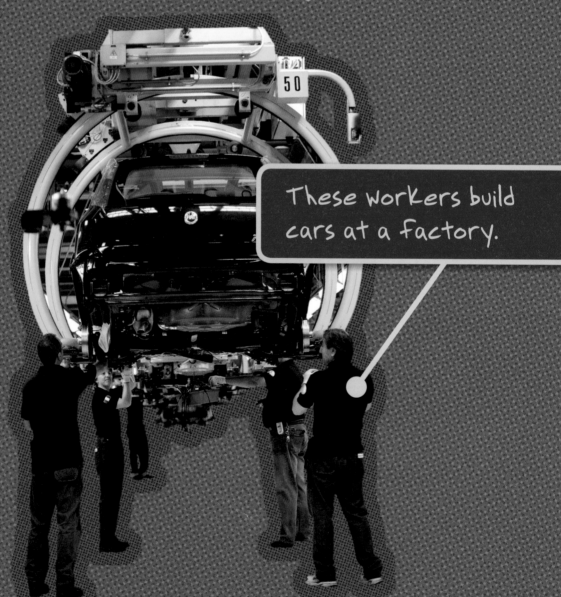

These workers build cars at a factory.

The ways people work have changed over time.

People at Work

In the past, women could not have certain jobs. Most law schools and medical schools did not accept women.

Many women worked as secretaries. One of their jobs was to write letters.

These days, women choose from many different jobs.

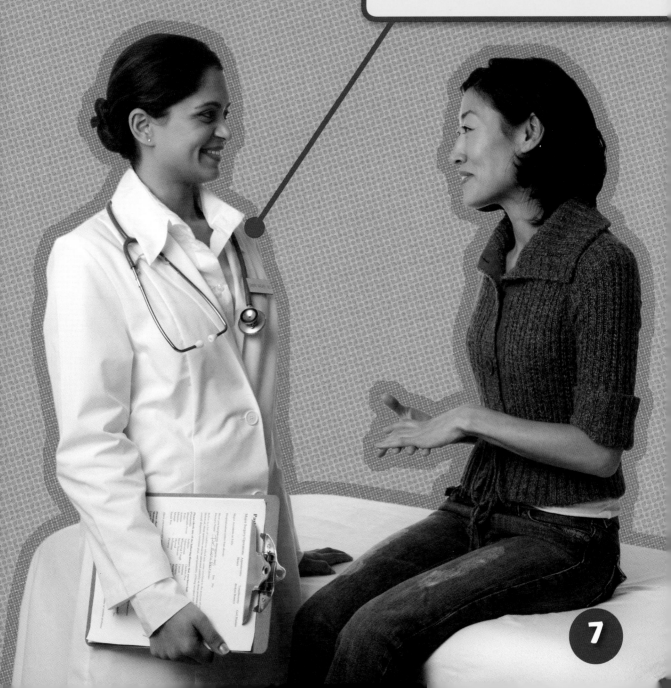

This woman works as a doctor.

In the past, many children earned money for their families. They worked instead of going to school.

Kids often worked long hours. Many jobs were dangerous.

These days, children must attend school. Laws protect children who work.

These child actors can work only a few hours a day. They must also finish schoolwork.

In the past, many teenagers worked after school. Some pumped gas or delivered newspapers.

These days, teenagers still work after school. Some work at stores or in restaurants.

In most cases, a person can work only after he or she turns fourteen.

Volunteers do
not earn money
for their work.

Teenagers often work as
volunteers. Volunteers help
others and learn new skills.

How Work Has Changed

New technology has made work faster and safer.

Special machines complete difficult or dangerous jobs.

In the past, farmers milked cows by hand.

These days, milking machines milk many cows at once.

In the past, construction workers wore regular clothes.

These days, construction workers wear some special clothing. The clothes make workers safer.

This worker's boots have metal in the soles to protect his feet.

In the past,
workers used
machines called
typewriters to
type messages.
Other people
often delivered
the messages.

These days, workers type
e-mails with computers.
They send these messages
over the Internet.

Many workers
send e-mails from
their cell phones.

In the past, people worked in lots of different places. Some worked on assembly lines in factories. Others worked in office buildings.

On an assembly line, each worker adds a separate part to the product that comes by.

These days, many people still work in factories or offices. Other people work from their homes. They have rooms called home offices.

New and Old Jobs

Many jobs of the past are no longer needed. Many jobs of the present are new. Some jobs have new names.

Elevator operators used to run elevators in stores and hotels.

In the past, pinsetters picked up bowling pins after a ball knocked them down. These days, bowling alleys have machines that pick up pins.

In the past, telephone operators connected people's phone calls.

Sound from each call traveled through wires.

These days, people work for cell phone companies. They use computers and satellites to help people talk to one another.

A worker makes repairs to a cell phone tower. The equipment on these towers helps cell phones work.

In the past, women worked as stewardesses. They helped airplane passengers.

These days, both men and women help passengers. They are called flight attendants.

Many things about work have changed over time. But our need for work has not changed.

Names to Know

These people helped change how people work in the United States.

Elizabeth Blackwell: Elizabeth Blackwell was the first woman to graduate from a U.S. medical school. She treated patients in the United States and Europe. In 1853, she opened a hospital for women and children. Later, she opened a medical college for female students.

James D. Hodgson: James D. Hodgson was the U.S. secretary of labor from 1970 to 1973. His job was to look out for the safety of American workers. He helped to pass the Occupational Safety and Health Act into law in 1970. This law improved workplace safety.

Mary Harris Jones: Mary Harris Jones helped workers protest (speak out against) dangerous jobs. She believed children belonged in school instead of at work.  In 1903, she led a protest march with child workers from mills and mines. She earned the nickname Mother Jones because she stood up for children.

Sally Ride: Sally Ride was the first American woman to fly in space. She joined the U.S. space program in 1978. She worked on the space shuttle *Challenger.* Her mission launched on June 18, 1983. She flew on another mission in October 1984.

Glossary

construction: the act of building or making something such as a house, a road, or an office building

job: a task that someone does regularly to get money

law: a rule that people must follow

satellite: an object that circles Earth and sends signals

technology: tools and methods that make tasks easier

typewriter: a machine used to print letters onto a sheet of paper

volunteer: a person who works without earning money

Further Reading

Heinz, Brian. *Nathan of Yesteryear and Michael of Today.* Minneapolis: Millbrook Press, 2007.

Kids Next Door: What's My Job?
http://www.hud.gov/kids/whatsjob.html

National Museum of American History: Women in Business
http://americanhistory.si.edu/archives/WIB-tour/mainMovie.html

Nelson, Robin. *Working Then and Now.* Minneapolis: Lerner Publications Company, 2008.

PBS Kids GO! Number Please: Connect with the First Telephone Operators
http://pbskids.org/wayback/tech1900/phone.html

Swinburne, Stephen R. *Whose Shoes? A Shoe for Every Job.* Honesdale, PA: Boyds Mills Press, 2010.

Index

Photo Acknowledgments

The images in this book are used with the permission of: © alexwhite/Shutterstock Images, p. 2; © Tips RM/Glow Images, p. 4; © SuperStock, pp. 5 (top), 14, 26 (top); © Jim Craigmyle/Corbis/Flirt/Glow Images, p. 5 (bottom); © Carsten/Hulton Archive/Getty Images, p. 6; © Iofoto/Shutterstock Images, p. 7; © Lewis Wickes Hine/Bettman/Corbis, p. 8; © Shaun Higson colour/Alamy, p. 9; © Peter Sickles/SuperStock, p. 10; © Catherine Karnow/Corbis, p. 11; © Catchlight Visual Services/Alamy, p. 12; © Imagebroker.net/SuperStock, p. 13; © Helen King/Corbis, p. 15; © Science and Society/SuperStock, p. 16; © IndexStock/SuperStock, p. 17; © Archive Photos/FPG/Getty Images, p. 18; © Yellow Dog Productions/The Image Bank/Getty Images, p. 19; © Courtesy CSU Archives/Everett Collection Inc/Alamy, p. 20; © LWA/Sharie Kennedy/Blend Images/Getty Images, p. 21; © Hulton Archive/Stringer/Getty Images, p. 22; National Archives, p. 23; © Charles E. Rotkin/Corbis, p. 24; © Paul Prescott/Shutterstock Images, p. 25; © David R. Frazier/Photolibrary Inc./Alamy, p. 26 (bottom); Courtesy John Deere & Company, p. 27; © Everett Collection/SuperStock, p. 29 (top); © Ron Lindsey/PhotoTake Inc./Alamy, p. 29 (bottom); © Sevalijevic/Shutterstock Images, p. 30; © Eye Ubiquitous/SuperStock, p. 31.

Front cover: Minneapolis Star Tribune, Minnesota Historical Society (top); © Monkey Business Images/Shutterstock Images (bottom).

Main body text set in Johann Light 30/36.